# THE APPALOOSA HORSE

By Ellen Frazel

Consultant:
Dr. Emily Leuthner
DVM, MS, DACVIM
Country View Veterinary Service
Oregon, Wisc.

BELLWETHER MEDIA • MINNEAPOLIS, MN

Jump into the cockpit and take flight with Pilot Books. Your journey will take you on high-energy adventures as you learn about all that is wild, weird, fascinating, and fun!

This edition first published in 2012 by Bellwether Media, Inc.

No part of this publication may be reproduced in whole or in part without written permission of the publisher. For information regarding permission, write to Bellwether Media, Inc., Attention: Permissions Department, 5357 Penn Avenue South, Minneapolis, MN 55419.

Library of Congress Cataloging-in-Publication Data

Frazel, Ellen.
  The Appaloosa horse / by Ellen Frazel.
     p. cm. – (Pilot books. Horse breed roundup)
  Includes bibliographical references and index.
  Summary: "Engaging images accompany information about the Appaloosa Horse. The combination of high-interest subject matter and narrative text is intended for students in grades 3 through 7"–Provided by publisher.
  ISBN 978-1-60014-655-8 (hardcover : alk. paper)
  1. Appaloosa horse–Juvenile literature. I. Title.
  SF293.A7F73 2012
  636.1'3–dc22                                        2011011673

Printed in the United States of America, North Mankato, MN.

080111       1187

# CONTENTS

# The Appaloosa Horse

The Wild West show has come to town! People of all ages gather to watch, and excitement fills the air. Out gallops a spotted horse carrying the famous Buffalo Bill. The crowd stands up and cheers. Buffalo Bill and other cowboys perform tricks with their horses and act out famous battles from the Western **frontier**. In one scene, Buffalo Bill and his cowboys chase **outlaws** who are trying to rob a train. They ride their strong, fast horses to catch the outlaws and save the day!

Buffalo Bill favored Appaloosas when he chose horses for his show. His own horse was an Appaloosa named Sultan. The horses made the Wild West show a major attraction across the United States in the 1800s. Today, Appaloosas can be seen all over the world. The breed is best known for its spotted coat patterns. This group of coat patterns is called the **leopard complex**. It is caused by certain **genes**. The spots on Appaloosas often look like those on a leopard or a Dalmatian.

## Rough Riders

The Congress of Rough Riders of the World performed in the Wild West show. This was a group of the best shooters from around the world!

Appaloosas have a few defining physical features. They have **mottled** skin around their eyes and lips. They also have stripes on their hooves. Appaloosa coats have many different color combinations and patterns. Some are all one color, but most are spotted. Coats with spots have a **base** and a **blanket**. The blanket color sits on top of the base color. It often covers the horse's hips and rear like a blanket.

**blanket with spots pattern**

An Appaloosa with a blanket pattern has a dark base with a white blanket. This horse is also called a snowcap Appaloosa. The blanket with spots pattern describes a coat with a white blanket that is spotted by the dark color of the base. Appaloosas with the leopard pattern have dark spots all over their white bodies.

Another coat pattern is roan. A roan Appaloosa has a mixture of light and dark hairs throughout its coat. Some Appaloosas have the roan blanket pattern. These horses have the roan pattern on only a portion of their bodies. Other Appaloosas have a roan blanket with spots.

No matter their coat pattern, Appaloosas are known for their intelligence and independent, trustworthy **temperament**. They like to be challenged and learn new things. It's a joy to train and ride these tough, spotted horses!

roan pattern

# Spotted Horses and the Nez Perce

Spotted horses have appeared in many cultures throughout history. Thousands of years ago, people in France drew pictures of spotted horses on the walls of caves. The Chinese told stories of spotted horses for hundreds of years. They spoke of their speed and bravery in battle. People called them "Heavenly Horses." In the 1200s, the great **Mongol** warrior Genghis Khan used spotted horses to conquer much of Asia and Europe.

Spanish explorers brought spotted horses to the Americas in the early 1500s. These horses are the **ancestors** of the Appaloosa. Native American tribes soon began using the spotted horses. The Nez Perce were skilled horsemen and warriors. They developed the Appaloosa breed by choosing the fastest and smartest horses to have **foals**. The Nez Perce used these quick, strong horses to hunt buffalo and attack enemies.

Genghis Khan

European **settlers** started exploring the land of what is now Washington and Idaho in the 1800s. They wandered into the Palouse River Valley, where the Nez Perce lived. The spotted horses of the Nez Perce fascinated the settlers. They called this type of horse "A Palouse Horse." This name changed over time to "Palousey," "Appalousey," and finally "Appaloosa."

In the late 1800s, the Nez Perce began to have conflicts with the United States government over land. Chief Joseph, the Nez Perce leader, set out in 1877 to lead 700 of his people to safety in Canada. The U.S. **cavalry** chased after them but could not keep up with the fast Appaloosas. The cavalry finally caught up when Chief Joseph and his people stopped to rest. Chief Joseph was forced to surrender, and the cavalry took the Nez Perce's horses. They sold many and hunted those that escaped. They feared the Appaloosa's speed, intelligence, and strong bond with the Nez Perce.

Chief Joseph

By 1938, Appaloosas were on the verge of **extinction**. A farmer named Claude Thompson decided to save the breed. He founded the Appaloosa Horse Club (ApHC) and gathered the remaining horses together to have foals. Today, the ApHC is located in Idaho and has **registered** more than 700,000 Appaloosas from around the world.

**Butch Cassidy**

### Getaway Horse

The outlaw Butch Cassidy owned one of the few Appaloosas that survived after 1877. He robbed banks and trains throughout Utah and rode away on his fast horse!

The ApHC holds the Chief Joseph Trail Ride every year to remember what happened in 1877. This ride is usually held in July or August. It covers about 100 miles (161 kilometers) of the path that Chief Joseph and the Nez Perce traveled. This ride usually takes a whole week to complete. Each year, up to 300 riders participate to support the Appaloosa breed!

# Polo, Competitions, and Breed Shows

Today, Appaloosas are suited for both work and play. People use them to ride along scenic trails or do work on ranches. People enjoy playing the sport of polo with Appaloosas. Players ride on horseback and try to hit a ball with long, wooden mallets. They score a point if they hit the ball into the other team's goal.

Appaloosas also do well in various competitions. In show jumping, they soar over hurdles and fences. Their intelligence and cooperation help them follow commands from their riders. In fox hunting, hunters on horseback follow dogs that are trained to track the scent of foxes. Appaloosas do well in both of these competitions because of their speed and **athleticism**.

jumping competition

## Movie Stars

Appaloosas have appeared on the big screen! In the Western movie *El Dorado*, John Wayne rode an Appaloosa. Matt Damon's horse in the movie *True Grit* was also an Appaloosa.

# Famous Appaloosas

## Sundance F-500

Sundance F-500 was a famous leopard Appaloosa born in 1932. He worked as a ranch horse and was known as one of the smartest Appaloosas in the country. He could untie a handkerchief, play dead, and shake hands. Sundance was the 500th horse registered with the ApHC.

## We Go Easy

Born in 1973, We Go Easy became a famous racehorse at just two years old. In 1975, she won six of the eight races she ran. She is most famous for her win in 1976 against a famous Thoroughbred sprinter called Right Pocket. She proved that Appaloosas were just as fast as Thoroughbreds or American Quarter Horses.

## The Executive

The Executive was a brownish gold Appaloosa born in 1973. He had a beautiful white blanket. He won the race for two-year-old horses at the National Horse Show in 1975. He also won every class but one in the Appaloosa horse breed show. The Executive fathered a total of 301 foals. Many of these horses went on to become champions as well. The Executive became part of the ApHC Hall of Fame in 1994.

The ApHC holds special **breed shows** for Appaloosas to compete in many different games, activities, and events. The Nez Perce Stake Race is one event. It is a form of **pole bending.** Many other horse breeds participate in pole bending, but the Nez Perce Stake Race is unique to the Appaloosa.

In most pole bending competitions, only one rider competes at a time. The Nez Perce Stake Race has two riders racing side by side. The horses weave around six poles arranged in a line. They must be careful not to knock any down. This event comes from games that the Nez Perce used to play with their horses. The race honors the rich history of the Appaloosa, an energetic breed loved by many today.

21

# Glossary

**ancestors**—family members who lived long ago

**athleticism**—good physical condition for activities involving speed, strength, and skill

**base**—the color that covers a horse's coat

**blanket**—the color that sits on top of a horse's base color; the blanket color often covers the hips and rear of a horse.

**breed shows**—shows in which horses compete to best represent their breed

**cavalry**—military troops on horseback

**extinction**—when every member of a species or breed has died

**foals**—young horses; foals are under one year old.

**frontier**—unexplored wilderness on the edge of settled land; the West was the great frontier of the United States in the 1800s.

**genes**—parts of DNA in living beings; genes produce specific physical characteristics.

**leopard complex**—a group of spotted coat patterns found in certain horse breeds; the leopard complex is caused by certain genes.

**Mongol**—a member of a nomadic group of people in Asia; Mongols now live mostly in Mongolia, China, and Russia.

**mottled**—having white or yellowish spots; Appaloosas usually have mottled skin around their eyes and mouth.

**outlaws**—people who have broken the law and not been caught

**pole bending**—an event where horses race along a course with six poles arranged in a line; the horses must weave between the poles as fast as they can without knocking them over.

**registered**—made record of; owners register their horses with official breed organizations.

**settlers**—people who come to live in a new land

**temperament**—behavior or nature; the Appaloosa has an independent, trustworthy temperament.

# To Learn More

## At the Library

O'Brien, Kim. *Appaloosa Horses*. Mankato, Minn.: Capstone Press, 2010.

Pavia, Audrey. *Appaloosa Spirit*. Irvine, Calif.: Bowtie Press, 1998.

Wedekind, Annie. *Wild Blue: The Story of a Mustang Appaloosa*. New York, N.Y.: Feiwel and Friends, 2009.

## On the Web

Learning more about Appaloosas is as easy as 1, 2, 3.

1. Go to www.factsurfer.com.

2. Enter "Appaloosas" into the search box.

3. Click the "Surf" button and you will see a list of related Web sites.

With factsurfer.com, finding more information is just a click away.

# Index

The images in this book are reproduced through the courtesy of: Mark J. Barrett / Alamy, front cover, pp. 18-19; Ron Kimball / KimballStock, pp. 4-5; Ellwood Eppard, pp. 6-7; imagebroker rf / Photolibrary, pp. 8-9; Public Domain, p. 10 (small); Nativestock Pictures / Photolibrary, pp. 10-11, 14-15; Getty Images, pp. 12 (small), 14 (small); Shattil & Rozinski / naturepl.com, pp. 12-13; Margo Harrison, pp. 16-17; Daryl Ann Anderson, pp. 20-21.